E•Z LEGAL FORMS®

... when you need it in writing!™

Do-It-Yourself Kit

Living Trust

INSTRUCTION MANUAL

E•Z LEGAL FORMS®
Deerfield Beach, Florida 33442

Revised 2/95

IMPORTANT FACTS

E-Z Legal Products are designed to provide authoritative and accurate information in regard to the subject matter covered. However, neither this nor any other publication can take the place of an attorney on important legal matters.

Information in this product has been carefully compiled from sources believed to be reliable, but the accuracy of the information is not guaranteed, as laws and regulations may change or be subject to differing interpretations. Additionally, certain courts may have their own requirements. Before completing and filing the forms in this kit, you may want to check with the clerk of the court concerning these requirements.

Why not have your attorney review this product? We encourage it.

LIMITED WARRANTY AND DISCLAIMER

This is a self-help legal product and is intended to be used by the consumer for his or her own benefit. Use of this product to benefit a second party may be considered the unauthorized practice of law.

As with any legal matter, common sense should determine whether you need the assistance of an attorney. We urge you to consult with an attorney whenever substantial amounts of money are involved or on any matter when you do not understand how to properly complete a form or question its adequacy to protect you.

It is understood that by using this legal product you are acting as your own attorney. Accordingly, the publisher, author, distributor and retailer shall have neither liability nor responsibility to any party for any loss or damage caused or alleged to be caused by use of this product. This product is sold with the understanding that the publisher, author, distributor and retailer are not engaged in rendering legal services. If legal services or other expert assistance are required, the services of a competent professional should be sought.

E-Z Legal Forms offers you a limited guarantee. If you consider E-Z Legal Forms to be defective in any way you may return your purchase and sales receipt to us within 30 days for a full refund of the list or purchase price, whichever is lower. In no event shall our liability—or the liability of any retailer—exceed the purchase price of the product. Use of the product constitutes acceptance of these terms.

00155

PRINTED IN THE UNITED STATES OF AMERICA

E•Z LEGAL FORMS®

384 S. Military Trail
Deerfield Beach, FL 33442
Tel. 305-480-8933 Fax 305-480-8906

TABLE OF CONTENTS

How to use E–Z Legal Kits

This E-Z Legal Kit can help you achieve an important legal objective conveniently, efficiently and economically. But it is nevertheless important for you to use this kit properly if you are to avoid later difficulties.

You can conveniently use this E-Z Legal Kit by following these step-by-step instructions:

1. Carefully read all information and instructions concerning the legal forms in this kit. If after thorough examination you decide that you have circumstances that are not covered by the forms in this kit, or you do not feel confident about writing your own documents, by all means do consult an attorney.

2. Complete each blank on each legal form. Do not skip over inapplicable blanks or lines intended to be completed. If the blank is inapplicable, mark "N/A" or "None" or use a dash. This shows you have not overlooked the item.

3. Always use pen or type on legal documents – never pencil.

4. Avoid erasures and "cross-outs" on final documents. Use a photocopy of each document as a worksheet.

5. Correspondence forms may be reproduced on your own letterhead if your prefer.

6. Whenever legal documents are to be executed by a partnership or corporation, the signatory should designate his or her title.

7. It is important to remember that on legal contracts or agreements between parties, all terms and conditions must be clearly stated. Provisions may not be enforceable unless in writing. All parties to the agreement should receive a copy.

8. You will find more specific instructions within this kit for completing some forms. These instructions are for your benefit and protection, so follow them closely.

9. You will find a helpful glossary of terms at the end of this booklet. Refer to this glossary if you encounter unfamiliar terms.

10. Always keep legal documents in a safe place and in a location known to your spouse, family, executor or attorney.

What is a Living Trust?

A *living trust* is one set up during your lifetime. A *testamentary trust,* in contrast, is one that comes into existence after your death.

Revocable *living trusts,* technically called revocable *inter vivos trusts,* are increasingly popular as a way to avoid probate. It is anticipated many more Americans will use a *living trust* in the years ahead.

A trust is an arrangement in which one person transfers property to a second person for the benefit of a third person. The person creating the trust is called the *grantor.* The person holding legal title to the trust property is the *trustee,* and the person for whose benefit the trust is created is called the *beneficiary.* In some limited cases, the same person can be the grantor, trustee, and beneficiary all at the same time.

With a *revocable living trust,* the grantor places property in trust, naming himself or herself or some other person as trustee, or co-trustee, but reserving the right to revoke the trust so that the property can be returned to the grantor. Generally, the trust agreement provides that upon the death of the grantor the property shall go to the named beneficiaries. This automatically avoids all probate of the property. The primary purpose is the avoidance of the inefficient and expensive probate system. The use of a revocable *living trust* thus avoids the delays and costs typically involved with probate courts.

For example, suppose a married couple provide in their revocable *living trust* that all or part of their assets be held by them, as co-trustees, for their benefit during their lifetimes, and upon death of either spouse to transfer to the surviving spouse (or other named beneficiaries). Immediately upon the death of either spouse, the property would automatically revert to the surviving spouse, as sole trustee, thus avoiding probate. The surviving spouse would have the option to place the assets in another revocable trust with an adult child or other family member as co-trustee, and in that manner continue to avoid probate.

In a second example, suppose an unmarried person provides in a revocable *living trust* that his assets be held by himself and a third party, as co-trustees, for the grantor's benefit during his lifetime, and upon the death of the grantor to go to the named beneficiaries. Immediately upon the grantor's death, all legal interest in the property would automatically revert to the co-trustee, as the sole trustee, to be transferred as directed by the grantor in the trust. If the beneficiary is an adult, he or she could be co-trustee and, upon the grantor's death, would automatically have title to the property.

It is not difficult to see how the *living trust* works. The *living trust* is established by creating a trust document.

The trust document provides instructions for managing the trust property during your lifetime, and will also direct the distribution of your property held in trust upon your death. You enjoy all income from the trust assets during your lifetime. Moreover, you never lose control of your property because you can always terminate, modify or revoke the trust and reclaim the assets. The documents in this kit help you to create and manage your *living trust.*

Specific advantages of a Living Trust

The revocable *living trust* offers several important advantages over a traditional Will. To summarize, the specific advantages of a *living trust* are:

1. **Cuts Costs:** Probate costs can be exorbitant, particularly in the many states that award executor fees based on a percentage of the decedent's estate. Even if you have property outside the trust subject to probate, you'll save money because much of the work required of the executor of the Will was already accomplished when the trust was established.

2. **Saves Time:** Probate, like most court proceedings, can drag along for years. With a *living trust,* the property passes on to your named beneficiaries almost immediately.

3. **Assures Privacy:** Probate records are public. Anybody can gain access to your most personal information. *Living trusts* are completely private. No one can find out what you own, or who you're leaving it to.

4. **Avoids Multi-State Problems:** If you die with property in more than one state, separate probate proceedings must be conducted, which adds to the costs and delays of probate. This is avoided when the property is held in a *living trust.*

5. **Discourages Legal Challenges:** As a general rule, trusts are harder to contest than Wills. One reason is that trust assets are not frozen pending the outcome of a legal challenge. When a Will is contested, the assets cannot be distributed until the claim is resolved. This encourages litigation, as prospective plaintiffs know that beneficiaries would often prefer to settle rather than face protracted delays.

6. **Protects During Disability:** A most important but frequently overlooked reason for setting up a *living*

trust is to ensure that someone will be available to handle your financial and legal affairs if serious illness renders you incapable of managing affairs for yourself. If, for example, you became suddenly disabled, your financial affairs would be in limbo. No one could operate your business, buy or sell property or even withdraw funds from your bank. If your assets were owned by a trust, your trustee(s) would continue to manage these assets notwithstanding your disability.

What Living Trusts can't do

living trust is a valuable estate planning tool, but it is not the panacea for all legal and financial dilemmas. Here are some things a *living trust* **won't** do for you.

1. **A living trust doesn't always eliminate the need for a regular testamentary Will.**
   Although you may place all your property into a *living trust,* there may be assets outside the trust requiring probate, including assets you may not even know about. This may include certain intangible property (i.e., literary rights, etc.), or someone may owe you money, or you may have an assertable legal claim against someone. Moreover, you maybe a beneficiary under someone else's Will under administration. These and other assets are often overlooked when establishing the living trust. Whether you intentionally or unintentionally have these assets outside the *living trust,* they should be disposed of by will.

   A testamentary Will is also necessary to name a personal guardian of your minor children. This cannot be handled through a *living trust.*

   A Will is not required in instances when you have all your assets in a *living trust* and no minor children requiring the appointment of a guardian. Should it be necessary to prepare a will,use an *E-Z Legal Last Will and Testament Kit.*

2. **Living trusts do not save on taxes.**
   Assets in your *living trust* are included in your estate for estate tax purposes. Thus, a *living trust* does not offer estate tax savings. You can, however, include in the trust document any tax-saving provisions that could be included in a Will.

Similarly, income generated by assets in the *living trust* during your lifetime will be taxed to you just as if the assets were in your personal name.

There is one tax *disadvantage* to a *living trust*: Unlike a trust, an estate can choose any fiscal year it wants, while a trust is required to use a calendar year.

3. **Living trusts do not protect assets from creditors.** Because living trusts are fully revocable, creditors of the grantor can reach the assets held in the *living trust*. Under certain conditions an *irrevocable trust* offers protection against creditors.

You can learn more about the use of trusts in asset protection by reading *Asset Protection Secrets*, a publication available from E-Z Legal Forms.

Living Trusts and your Will

What would happen if you placed an asset such as a stock certificate in a *living trust* and either earlier or later bequeathed the same stock certificate under your will?

Here, the revocable *living trust* takes precedence over the Will because title (ownership) of the asset was *immediately* transferred when the trust was established, while the Will does not become operative until death.

For this reason, you should not anticipate leaving in your Will property that is placed under the *living trust.*

If you do leave property **outside** your *living trust,* you should consider a "pour over" Will to accompany your *living trust.* With a "pour over" Will, you have a catchall whereby miscellaneous assets will, upon your death, be transferred to your *living trust* for distribution. Bear in mind that this still defeats the purpose of a *living trust,* as these assets remain subject to probate.

Living Trusts and joint ownership

Many people believe they can avoid probate and achieve the benefits of a *living trust* by placing their property under joint ownership. Upon the death of one joint owner, the other takes the property automatically without probate proceedings. Joint ownership is an alternative to a *living trust*, but there are three disadvantages to joint ownership:

1. You may lose control of your property if your joint owner doesn't agree with your plans to, for example, sell or mortgage the property. You may also lose the property to a creditor of your joint owner.

2. Joint ownership is not appropriate for all property. Motor vehicles are one example.

3. If your transferee is anyone but a spouse, there may be gift tax problems. Further, if one joint owner dies, the IRS may tax the full value of the property to that individual's estate – requiring the surviving owner to prove he paid consideration for his or her interest.

Each of these potential problems can be avoided with a *living trust,* since you: 1) always retain full control of your property, 2) can use it for any type of property, and 3) never face adverse tax consequences with a *living trust.*

Living Trusts and marital property rights

Most states grant certain legal rights to a surviving spouse that cannot be defeated by a will. These rights – frequently called community property, dower, curtesy, statutory or elective rights – typically give one-half or one-third of the estate to the surviving spouse, notwithstanding the terms of a will or existence of a *living trust.* Thus, *living trusts* are not an effective vehicle for the denial of rights to a spouse. It is thus necessary in these states to leave your spouse an amount (usually one-third) at least equal to the minimum percentage of your estate as required by statute.

Dower and/or curtesy rights exist in these states:

Hawaii

Kentucky

Massachusetts

Michigan

Ohio

Vermont

If you are married and do **not** designate your spouse as a trust beneficiary, and live in one of these states, you should consult with an attorney concerning the validity of your provisions.

Community property laws create different problems concerning the handling of trusts and estates. Community property laws are in effect in:

Arizona	Nevada
California	New Mexico
Idaho	Washington
Louisiana	Wisconsin

If you live in a state with "community property" laws, you should also consult an attorney.

Selecting Trustees for your Living Trust

You can operate a living trust with either one or two trustees (co-trustees). The grantor should consider a co-trustee, particularly if an adult beneficiary (i.e., adult child or spouse) is a primary or sole beneficiary.

You can appoint yourself as trustee and appoint one or more co-trustees. If you name an individual co-trustee (instead of a financial institution), be certain to name one or more alternatives. This is advantageous in the event one trustee is incapable or unwilling to act. You can also allow your trustee to name his or her own successor. You can also name yourself as trustee. This is preferred by most individuals, as it allows them continuous control over the management of the trust assets.

The powers of the trustees are to:

a) manage, sell, encumber, pledge, lease or invest the trust property.

b) pay to the grantor(s) any sums requested by the grantor(s).

c) distribute the trust assets.

Be certain to carefully review the responsibilities with a prospective trustee *before* appointment. The trustee must also be mindful that he or she owes a fiduciary duty to both the grantor and beneficiaries, and therefore must prudently manage the trust assets, avoiding conflict or undisclosed personal gain.

Whether a trustee is compensated for his or her services is strictly a matter of agreement between the trustee and grantors. Obviously, it is a matter best resolved *before* the trustee is named. You can, of course, best sidestep the expense of a trustee by appointing yourself or your spouse as trustee.

What property can be placed in Living Trust?

It is not sufficient simply to prepare a *living trust*. There must be an actual transfer of property to the trust. Property is transferred from the grantor to the trust in the same manner it would be transferred to any other third party.

- ► Personal property is transferred by bill of sale.
- ► Real estate is transferred by deed.
- ► Stocks and bonds must be sent to the transfer agents to be put in the trust's name.

The following are a few assets that are best left **outside** the trust.

- ► *Personal checking accounts* should be kept in your name for day-to-day expenditures.
- ► *Retirement accounts* should not be transferred to the trust. Any transfer of IRA's, Keogh's, company pensions or other qualified retirement accounts is deemed a *taxable* distribution.
- ► *Life insurance* can be owned by the trust. However, you can have the proceeds escape estate taxes by establishing a separate life insurance trust.
- ► *Shares of stock in a Subchapter S corporation* cannot be owned by a *living trust*. For a corporation to qualify as a Subchapter S corporation, its shares must be owned only by individuals.

The most common error is to leave property outside the *living trust* needlessly, thus subjecting it to probate. Use this checklist as you review property you may consider for transfer:

- antiques
- artwork
- copyrights
- trademarks
- patents
- boats
- airplanes
- business interests
- vacation home
- personal residence
- shares of stock
- bonds
- investments
- real estate
- bank accounts
- collectibles
- certificates of deposit
- investment securities
- cash
- life insurance policies

- automobiles
- recreational equipment
- household furnishings
- jewelry
- other vehicles
- proceeds of IRA's and Keogh's
- employee benefits

Assets may be transferred into the living trust *simultaneous* with its execution. This is accomplished by attaching to the *living trust* a schedule of property.

It is also possible to transfer property into the living trust at a later date. In fact, it is quite important that later acquisitions be made in the name of the trust. This will again avoid the inadvertent accumulation of property outside the trust that will trigger probate.

Keep accurate written records of property transferred into and out of the trust. Respect the fact that the living trust is a separate entity.

Managing your Living Trust

A common concern is that the *living trust* will be burdensome to administer. This worry is generally unfounded. A *living trust* can be managed quite easily and with surprisingly little paperwork.

Aside from drafting your *living trust* and transferring your assets to it, you have only three other basic responsibilities:

1. **Keep simple records:**
   It is important to remember that although you may continue to fully control the trust property, the *living trust* is nevertheless a separate entity. As such you must keep adequate records to reflect:

   a) property transferred to and from the trust.

   b) income earned by the trust.

   c) expenses and disbursements paid or incurred by the trust.

2. **Maintain a separate checking account:**
   Never co-mingle trust funds with your own. Operate a separate checking account for your trust. Your bank can help you set up a trust checking account. Be careful to follow the proper formalities when signing

checks under the trust account. Thus, all checks, for example, will be signed:

Mary Jones Trust

by______________________________
Mary Jones, Trustee

You should use the same signing format on all documents when you act on behalf of the trust.

3. **Insure the trust property:**
Because trust property is owned by the trust, the property must be insured in the name of the trust. Coordinate insurance coverage with your insurance agent whenever you place property into the *living trust.*

How are Living Trusts taxed?

Generally, a *living trust* poses no special tax problems. Here, however, are some pointers on the most commonly asked questions:

1. *Is there a taxable consequence when property is transferred into the trust?*
No. The trust takes the property at the grantor's basis, so no taxable consequence arises. The transfer of securities to or from a *living trust* may incur a securities transfer tax in some states. If you plan to transfer substantial amounts of stock, check first with your accountant or attorney.

2. *Is it necessary for the trust to file its own tax return?*
There is no need to get a separate taxpayer identification number for the trust or file a fiduciary income tax return as long as you appoint yourself or your spouse as trustee.

3. *What tax problems arise if the trust is set up in a state other than where the grantor resides?*
There is a possibility of double state income taxation should you set up a *living trust* in another state. This problem can be resolved by setting up the trust in the state where you reside. Should you move to another state, you can amend the *living trust* to reflect that it will be governed by the laws of your new state.

4. *Can a living trust be used when assets exceed $600,000?* A *living trust* can be used for any size estate. However, if you are married and your gross estate exceeds $600,000 (including *living trust* property) then you should consult a tax attorney. You may minimize your estate taxes by having you and your spouse set up separate reciprocal *living trusts,* often called "A and B Trusts."

5. *Does a living trust affect personal income taxes?* A *living trust* does not change your personal income tax obligation. Even when income (i.e., a personal paycheck) is deposited directly into the trust, you must still report and pay taxes on the income. Similarly, you can personally deduct tax-deductible expenses, notwithstanding their payment from the trust.

Rights to the Living Trust property

A chief advantage of the *living trust* is that the grantor continues to fully control the trust property *until* his or her death. Only then is the trust property transferred to the beneficiaries named in the trust. This means that during the grantor's life, the grantor continues to enjoy all income generated by the trust and also retains the right to use all or any part of the trust principal for his or her own needs.

Because you are a trustee during your lifetime (or have the right to change the trustee or even revoke the trust), you can:

- sell or gift property in the trust
- mortgage or borrow against the trust property
- add property to the trust
- retransfer to yourself property in the trust
- change beneficiaries

Caution: Should you and your spouse establish the trust jointly, you must **both** consent to any changes, although either of you can revoke the trust.

Because the beneficiaries enjoy no rights to the trust property until the death of the grantor, they are entitled to neither income nor principal until death of the grantor occurs. Similarly, no creditor of a beneficiary can attach the interest of the beneficiary until it passes to the beneficiary. Creditors of the grantor can attach the trust property before the death of the grantor. Since the trustee only holds title to the trust asset on behalf of the grantor, the trust property is safe from creditors of the trustee unless the trustee is also the grantor.

Naming beneficiaries

Naming beneficiaries to the *living trust* is similar to the process of preparing your will.

As with a will, you can designate specific property to specific beneficiaries or, alternatively, you may leave beneficiaries a fixed percentage or all of the property in the trust.

Bear in mind that trust property is "sole and separate" property when transferred to the beneficiary, unless, of course, the beneficiaries are husband and wife.

Examples of how beneficiaries may be named are as follows:

a) if a single beneficiary:

> *"To John Smith, as his sole and separate property."*

b) if two or more beneficiaries:

> *"To John Smith and Rachel Brown (etc.) in equal shares, as their sole and separate property."*

c) if husband and wife are beneficiaries:

> *"To John Smith and Mildred Smith, husband and wife."*

d) if the guardian of a minor is beneficiary:

> *"To Henry Rogers, as guardian of Steven Brown, a minor child."*

You may also designate contingent beneficiaries in the event a first named beneficiary predeceases you.

e) *"In the event my son John shall predecease me, I leave his shares to his then surviving children, to share equally."*

As with a will, it is important to review your designated beneficiaries periodically so that the trust is always up to date and accurately reflects how you want to leave your property.

Recording the Living Trust

If the trust is to hold real estate it will be necessary to file and record the trust in the public records office where deeds are recorded.

Similarly, it will be necessary to record any change of trustees, modifications to the trust or revocation of the trust.

Also, several states have adopted the Uniform Probate Code. If you live in one of the following states, you must record your *living trust* with the probate court (or designated public office).

Alaska	Montana
Arizona	Nebraska
Colorado	New Mexico
Hawaii	North Dakota
Idaho	South Dakota
Michigan	Utah

In other states, recording the *living trust* is optional but highly recommended. Only through recording can third parties be assured that they are dealing with a trustee with the requisite authority to act on behalf of the trust.

Revoking or changing the Living Trust

The great advantage of the revocable *living trust* is that you have the ability, at any time, for any reason, or for no reason, to modify or revoke the trust. Thus, you never lose control of the property you transfer to the trust. With a stroke of the pen the trust can be revoked or changed.

The revocable living trust in this kit is automatically terminated upon death of the grantor. This is common in revocable living trusts. However a trust may contain a provision continuing the trust until the beneficiaries are 18 (or 21) years of age.

A trust also ceases to operate when there is no property, or *trust res*, within the trust.

Modification of the trust may involve:

1. Change of trustees
2. Addition or deletion of property
3. Change of beneficiaries
4. Change of trust terms

This kit contains necessary forms to either modify or revoke the *living trust.*

The Living Trust forms

This kit contains the following ready-to-use documents:

1. Revocable Living Trust
2. Assignment of Property to Trust
3. Schedule of Beneficiaries
4. Schedule of Assets
5. Amendment to Trust
6. Revocation of Trust

GLOSSARY OF USEFUL TERMS

Administrator – A person the court appoints to manage the probate of the estate of a person without a valid will.

Beneficiary – A person or party named in a Will to receive a portion of the estate. A beneficiary may also be a person who receives payment from a life insurance policy or income from a trust.

Bequest – A gift of property made through a Will.

Codicil – An amendment to an original Will that changes or modifies the Will.

Contingent Beneficiary – A person designated to become a beneficiary if the first beneficiary predeceases the Testator.

Estate – All property owned by a person at death. This includes both real and personal property.

Executor – A person named by the Testator in a Will to administer the estate.

Guardian – A person with legal control and responsibility for a minor child or an incompetent adult.

Heir – A person who inherits property, either through a Will or intestate succession.

Intestate – A person who dies without leaving a valid Will.

Joint Property – All property owned jointly with another party or parties.

Living Trust – A trust established while alive, also known as an *inter vivos* trust.

Living Will – A signed, witnessed statement requesting that life not be prolonged by artificial means should death become inevitable.

Personal Property – All property owned by a person except real property. Personal property can include bank accounts, automobiles, boats, planes, stock, bonds, heirlooms and other personal effects.

Probate – The process of proving the legality and validity of a Will in court.

Real Property – All real estate (land, improvements, buildings), including residences, commercial property, vacation property, farms, condominiums and time-share units.

Remainder – What's left of an estate after specific property is distributed.

Revoke – To cancel or terminate the Will or certain provisions of the Will.

Surety Bond – A bond should the administrator improperly administer the probate of the estate, thereby creating losses.

Tax Base – The taxable value of property at the time of transfer.

Testator – A person who makes a valid Will.

Trust – An agreement in which a person transfers property to a trustee to hold and manage for the benefit of another person (the trust beneficiary).

Trustee – The person who holds title, manages and distributes the trust property for the benefit of the trust beneficiary.

Will – A legal document that sets forth the wishes of the Testator after his or her death. This document distributes the property of the Testator and appoints representatives to administer the estate.

Witness – A person who verifies the signature of the Testator.

NOTES

AMENDMENT TO TRUST NO_______________

NAME OF TRUST:

Effective Date of Trust: Amendment Date:

Settlors/Grantors: Trustees:

(Hereinafter referred to as Settlors/Grantors) (Hereinafter referred to as Trustees)

The above-described trust, by and between the above-named Settlors/Grantors and Trustees, is amended by substituting provisions, adding provisions, or deleting the following provisions:

All provisions of the above trust are hereby incorporated by reference herein with the exception of the provisions expressly modified by this Amendment.

IN WITNESS WHEREOF, the parties hereto have duly executed this Amendment to the above Trust on date first above written.

______________________________ ______________________________

______________________________ ______________________________

Signature of Settlor/Grantor Signature of Trustee

This trust amendment was signed in the presence of us who, at the request and in the presence of Grantors and in the presence of each other, have signed as witnesses thereto.

Witnesses:

____

____

____

Signature of Witnesses

State of , 19

, SS

County of

Then personally appeared ,
Settlor/Grantor and ,
Trustee, who each acknowledged the foregoing, before me.

____

Notary Public
My Commission Expires:

ASSIGNMENT OF PROPERTY TO TRUST

Seller/Assignor: ,
does hereby sell, transfer and convey unto
, as Trustee(s) of
, a revocable living trust
dated , 19 .

The Property transferred consists of:

To have and to hold for the benefit of the trust, its beneficiaries, successors and assigns. Seller warrants to defend the sale of property against all and every person claiming an adverse interest to same.

Signed under seal this day of , 19 .

In presence of:

______________________________ ______________________________
Settlor/Assignor

REVOCABLE LIVING TRUST
Known as

____

Dated:_________________________________

Agreement made and executed this day of , 19 , by and between , hereinafter referred to as the Grantor, and , hereinafter referred to as the Trustee.

Grantor desires to create a revocable trust of the property described in Schedule A hereto annexed, together with such monies, and other assets as the Trustee may hereafter at any time hold or acquire hereunder (hereinafter referred to collectively as the "Trust Estate"), for the purposes hereinafter set forth.

NOW, THEREFORE, in consideration of the premises and of the mutual covenants herein contained, the Grantor agrees to execute such further instruments as shall be necessary to vest the Trustee with full title to the property, and the Trustee agrees to hold the Trust Estate, IN TRUST, NEVERTHELESS, for the following uses and purposes and subject to the terms and conditions hereinafter set forth:

The Trustee shall hold, manage, invest and reinvest the Trust Estate (if any requires such management and investment) and shall collect the income, if any, therefrom and shall dispose of the net income and principal as follows:

I

(1) During the lifetime of the Grantor, the Trustee shall pay to or apply for the benefit of the Grantor all the net income from the Trust.

(2) During the lifetime of the Grantor, the Trustee may pay to or apply for the benefit of the Grantor such sums from the principal of this Trust as in its sole discretion shall be necessary or advisable from time to time for the medical care, comfortable maintenance and welfare of the Grantor, taking into consideration to the extent the Trustee deems advisable, any other income or resources of the Grantor known to the Trustee.

(3) The Grantor may at any time during his lifetime and from time to time, withdraw all

or any part of the principal of this Trust, free of trust, by delivering an instrument in writing duly signed by him to the Trustee, describing the property or portion thereof desired to be withdrawn. Upon receipt of such instrument, the Trustee shall thereupon convey and deliver to the Grantor, free of trust, the property described in such instrument.

(4) In the event that the Grantor is adjudicated to be incompetent or in the event that the Grantor is not adjudicated incompetent, but by reason of illness or mental or physical disability is, in the opinion of the Trustee, unable to properly handle his own affairs, then and in that event the Trustee may during the Grantor's lifetime, in addition to the payments of income and principal for the benefit of the Grantor, pay to or apply for the benefit of any one or more of the Grantor's husband/wife, and the Grantor's minor children such sums from the net income and from the principal of this Trust in such shares and proportions as in its sole discretion it shall determine to be necessary or advisable from time to time for the medical care, comfortable maintenance and welfare of the Grantor's said husband/wife and children taking into consideration to the extent the Trustee deems advisable, any other income or resources of the Grantor's said husband/wife and minor children known to the Trustee.

(5) The interests of the Grantor shall be considered primary and superior to the interests of any beneficiary.

II

The Grantor reserves and shall have the exclusive right at any time and from time to time during his/her lifetime by instrument in writing signed by the Grantor and delivered to the Trustee to modify or alter this Agreement, in whole or in part, without the consent of the Trustee or any beneficiary provided that the duties, powers and liabilities of the Trustee shall not be changed without his/her consent; and the Grantor reserves and shall have the right during his/her lifetime, by instrument in writing, signed by the Grantor and delivered to the Trustee, to cancel and annul this Agreement without the consent of the Trustee or any beneficiary hereof. Grantor expressly reserves the right to appoint successor trustees, replace present trustees and change the beneficiaries or the rights to property due any beneficiary.

III

In addition to any powers granted under applicable law or otherwise, and not in limitation of such powers, but subject to any rights and powers which may be reserved expressly by the Grantor(s) in this Agreement, the Trustee(s) is/are authorized to exercise the following powers in their sole and absolute discretion.

a. To hold and retain any or all property, real, personal, or mixed, received from the Grantor's estate, or from any other source, regardless of any law or rule of court relating to diversification, or non-productivity, for such time as the Trustee shall deem best, and to dispose of such property by sale, exchange, or otherwise, as and when they shall deem advisable; notwithstanding this provision or any other contained herein.

b. To sell, assign, exchange, transfer, partition and convey, or otherwise dispose of, any property, real, personal or mixed, which may be included in or may at any time become part of the Trust Estate, upon such terms and conditions as deemed advisable, at either public or private sale, including options and sales on credit and for the purpose of selling, assigning, exchanging, transferring, partitioning or conveying the same, to make, execute, acknowledge, and deliver any and all instruments of conveyance, deeds of trust, and assignments in such form and with such warranties and covenants as they may deem expedient and proper; and in the event of any sale, conveyance or other disposition of any of the Trust Estate, the purchaser shall not be obligated in any way to see the application of the purchase money or other consideration passing in connection therewith.

c. To lease or rent and manage any or all of the real estate, which may be included in or at any time become a part of the Trust Estate, upon such terms and conditions deemed advisable, irrespective of whether the term of the lease shall exceed the period permitted by law or the probable period of any trust created hereby, and to review and modify such leases; and for the purpose of leasing said real estate, to make, execute, acknowledge and deliver any and all instruments in such form and with such covenants and warranties as they may deem expedient and proper; and to make any repairs, replacements, and improvements, structural and otherwise, of any property, and to charge the expense thereof in an equitable manner to principal or income, as deemed proper.

d. To borrow money for any purpose in connection with said Trust created hereby, and to execute promissory notes or other obligation for amounts so borrowed, and to secure the payment of any such amounts by mortgage or pledge or any real or personal property, and to renew or extend the time of payment of any obligation, secured or unsecured, payable to or by any trust created hereby, for such periods of time as deemed advisable.

e. To invest and reinvest or leave temporarily uninvested any or all of the funds of the Trust Estate as said Trustees in their sole discretion may deem best, including investments in stocks, common and preferred, and common trust fund, without being restricted to those investments expressly approved by statute for investment by fiduciaries, and to change investments from realty to personality, and vice versa.

f. To compromise, adjust, arbitrate, sue or defend, abandon, or otherwise deal with and settle claims, in favor of or against the Trust Estate as the Trustees shall deem best and their decision shall be conclusive.

g. To determine in a fair and reasonable manner whether any part of the Trust Estate, or any addition or increment thereto be income or principal, or whether any cost, charge, expense, tax, or assessment shall be charged against income or principal, or partially against income and partially against principal.

h. To engage and compensate, out of principal or income or both, as equitably determined, agents, accountants, brokers, attorneys-in-fact, attorneys-at-law, tax specialists, realtors, custodians, investment counsel, and other assistants and advisors, and to do so without liability for any neglect, omission, misconduct, or default of any such agent or such agent or professional representative, provided he or she was selected and retained with reasonable care.

i. To vote any stock, bonds, or other securities held by the Trust at any meetings of stockholders, bondholders, or other security holders and to delegate the power so to vote to attorneys-in-fact or proxies under power of attorney, restricted or unrestricted, and to join in or become a party to any organization, readjustment, voting trust, consideration or exchange, and to deposit securities with any persons, and to pay any fees incurred in connection therewith, and to charge the same to principal or income, as deemed proper, and to exercise all of the rights with regard to such securities.

j. To purchase securities, real estate, or other property from the executor or other personal representative of the Grantor's estate, the executor or other personal representative of the Grantor's husband's/wife's estate, and the Trustees of any agreement or declaration executed by the Grantor during his/her lifetime under his/her last will in case his/her executors or Trustees are in need of cash, liquid assets, or income-producing assets with which to pay taxes, claims, or other estate or trust indebtedness, or in case such executors or Trustees are in need of such property to properly exercise and discharge their discretion with respect to distributions to beneficiaries as provided for under such bills, declarations, or agreements. Such purchase may be in cash or may be in exchange for other property of this Trust, and the Trustees shall not be liable in any way for any loss resulting to the Trust Estate by reason of the exercise of said authority.

k. To undertake such further acts as are incidental to any of the foregoing or are reasonably required to carry out the tenor, purpose and intent of the Trust.

l. To make loans or advancements to the executor or other personal representative of the Grantor's estate, the executor or other personal representative of the Grantor's husband's/wife's estate, and the Trustees of any agreement or declaration executed by the Grantor during his/her lifetime or under his/her last will in case such executors or Trustees are in need of cash for any reason. Such loans or advancements may be secured or unsecured, and the Trustees shall not be liable in any way for any loss resulting to the Trust Estate by reason of the exercise of this authority.

IV

Upon death of the Grantor, or the last surviving Grantor if more than one, the remaining Trust assets shall be distributed to the beneficiaries in the proportionate or allocable amounts as are specified in the schedule of beneficiaries as may then be in force.

If any beneficiary and the Grantor should die under such circumstances as would render it doubtful whether the beneficiary or the Grantor died first, then it shall be conclusively presumed for the purposes of this Trust that said beneficiary predeceased the Grantor.

V

If it shall be determined that any provision of the Trust created herein violates any rule against perpetuities or remoteness of vesting now or hereafter in effect in a governing jurisdiction, that portion of the Trust herein created shall be administered as herein provided until the termination of the maximum period allowed by law at which time and forthwith such part of the Trust shall be distributed in fee simple to the beneficiaries then entitled to receive income therefrom, and for the purpose, it shall be presumed that any beneficiary entitled to receive support or education from the income or principal of any particular fund is entitled to receive the income therefrom.

VI

Except as otherwise provided herein, all payments of principal and income payable, or to become payable, to the beneficiary of any trust created hereunder shall not be subject to anticipation, assignment, pledge, sale or transfer in any manner, nor shall any said beneficiary have the power to anticipate or encumber such interest, nor shall such interest, while in possession of the Trustee, be liable for, or subject to, the debts, contracts obligations, liabilities or torts of any beneficiary.

VII

This Trust Agreement shall be construed, regulated and governed by and in accordance with the laws of the State of .

I certify that I have read the foregoing Trust Agreement and that it correctly states the terms and conditions under which the Trust Estate is to be held, managed and disposed of by the Trustee.

Dated:_______________________ ______________________________
Grantor

____
Trustee

State of }
County of

On before me, ,
appeared
personally known to me (or proved to me on the basis of satisfactory evidence) to be the person(s) whose name(s) is/are subscribed to the within instrument and acknowledged to me that he/she/they executed the same in his/her/their authorized capacity(ies), and that by his/her/their signature(s) on the instrument the person(s), or the entity upon behalf of which the person(s) acted, executed the instrument.
WITNESS my hand and official seal.

Signature_____________________________

Affiant _____Known _____Produced ID
Type of ID______________________
(Seal)

REVOCATION OF TRUST

We, the undersigned, , as Settlors/Grantors of a certain revocable living trust entitled , dated , 19 , do hereby revoke said trust effective this date.

1. Notice: A copy of this revocation has been mailed to the below-named trustee(s).

And a further copy of this revocation has been mailed to the below-named beneficiaries.

2. Recording: A signed original of this notice of revocation shall or has been duly recorded with the county recorders office in the following counties:

We make this revocation under oath and affirm that the facts stated herein are true and correct this day of , 19 .

______________________________	______________________________
Settlor/Grantor	Settlor/Grantor

State of }
County of

On before me, ,
appeared
personally known to me (or proved to me on the basis of satisfactory evidence) to be the person(s) whose name(s) is/are subscribed to the within instrument and acknowledged to me that he/she/they executed the same in his/her/their authorized capacity(ies), and that by his/her/their signature(s) on the instrument the person(s), or the entity upon behalf of which the person(s) acted, executed the instrument.
WITNESS my hand and official seal.

Signature________________________________

Affiant _____Known _____Produced ID
Type of ID_______________________
(Seal)

(Revised 3/93)

SCHEDULE OF ASSETS

Name of Trust:	Date of Trust:

No.	Date of Transfer In	Assets Transferred to Trust	Form of Ownership	Tax Base at Time of Transfer	Fair Market Value on Date of Transfer

No.	Date of Transfer Out	Assets Transferred From Trust	Form of Ownership	Tax Base at Time of Transfer	Fair Market Value on Date of Transfer

The undersigned Grantors have reviewed the Schedule of Assets and approve the form of ownership of property as set forth above this date:

_______________________________ _______________________________

Signature of Grantor/Settlor Signature of Grantor/Settlor

K105-5B

SCHEDULE OF BENEFICIARIES AND DISTRIBUTIVE SHARES

The following are the named beneficiaries of the Trust, as of this day of , 19 .

Name of Beneficiary	Property Distributed and Quantity and/or Percent

AMENDMENT TO TRUST NO______________

NAME OF TRUST:

Effective Date of Trust: Amendment Date:

Settlors/Grantors: Trustees:

(Hereinafter referred to as Settlors/Grantors) (Hereinafter referred to as Trustees)

The above-described trust, by and between the above-named Settlors/Grantors and Trustees, is amended by substituting provisions, adding provisions, or deleting the following provisions:

All provisions of the above trust are hereby incorporated by reference herein with the exception of the provisions expressly modified by this Amendment.

IN WITNESS WHEREOF, the parties hereto have duly executed this Amendment to the above Trust on date first above written.

_____________________________ _____________________________

_____________________________ _____________________________

Signature of Settlor/Grantor Signature of Trustee

This trust amendment was signed in the presence of us who, at the request and in the presence of Grantors and in the presence of each other, have signed as witnesses thereto.

Witnesses:

____

____

____

Signature of Witnesses

State of , 19

, SS

County of

Then personally appeared ,
Settlor/Grantor and ,
Trustee, who each acknowledged the foregoing, before me.

____

Notary Public
My Commission Expires:

ASSIGNMENT OF PROPERTY TO TRUST

Seller/Assignor: ,
does hereby sell, transfer and convey unto
, as Trustee(s) of
, a revocable living trust
dated , 19 .

The Property transferred consists of:

To have and to hold for the benefit of the trust, its beneficiaries, successors and assigns. Seller warrants to defend the sale of property against all and every person claiming an adverse interest to same.

Signed under seal this day of , 19 .

In presence of:

______________________________ ______________________________
Settlor/Assignor

REVOCABLE LIVING TRUST
Known as

____

Dated:_________________________________

Agreement made and executed this day of , 19 , by and between , hereinafter referred to as the Grantor, and , hereinafter referred to as the Trustee.

Grantor desires to create a revocable trust of the property described in Schedule A hereto annexed, together with such monies, and other assets as the Trustee may hereafter at any time hold or acquire hereunder (hereinafter referred to collectively as the "Trust Estate"), for the purposes hereinafter set forth.

NOW, THEREFORE, in consideration of the premises and of the mutual covenants herein contained, the Grantor agrees to execute such further instruments as shall be necessary to vest the Trustee with full title to the property, and the Trustee agrees to hold the Trust Estate, IN TRUST, NEVERTHELESS, for the following uses and purposes and subject to the terms and conditions hereinafter set forth:

The Trustee shall hold, manage, invest and reinvest the Trust Estate (if any requires such management and investment) and shall collect the income, if any, therefrom and shall dispose of the net income and principal as follows:

I

(1) During the lifetime of the Grantor, the Trustee shall pay to or apply for the benefit of the Grantor all the net income from the Trust.

(2) During the lifetime of the Grantor, the Trustee may pay to or apply for the benefit of the Grantor such sums from the principal of this Trust as in its sole discretion shall be necessary or advisable from time to time for the medical care, comfortable maintenance and welfare of the Grantor, taking into consideration to the extent the Trustee deems advisable, any other income or resources of the Grantor known to the Trustee.

(3) The Grantor may at any time during his lifetime and from time to time, withdraw all

or any part of the principal of this Trust, free of trust, by delivering an instrument in writing duly signed by him to the Trustee, describing the property or portion thereof desired to be withdrawn. Upon receipt of such instrument, the Trustee shall thereupon convey and deliver to the Grantor, free of trust, the property described in such instrument.

(4) In the event that the Grantor is adjudicated to be incompetent or in the event that the Grantor is not adjudicated incompetent, but by reason of illness or mental or physical disability is, in the opinion of the Trustee, unable to properly handle his own affairs, then and in that event the Trustee may during the Grantor's lifetime, in addition to the payments of income and principal for the benefit of the Grantor, pay to or apply for the benefit of any one or more of the Grantor's husband/wife, and the Grantor's minor children such sums from the net income and from the principal of this Trust in such shares and proportions as in its sole discretion it shall determine to be necessary or advisable from time to time for the medical care, comfortable maintenance and welfare of the Grantor's said husband/wife and children taking into consideration to the extent the Trustee deems advisable, any other income or resources of the Grantor's said husband/wife and minor children known to the Trustee.

(5) The interests of the Grantor shall be considered primary and superior to the interests of any beneficiary.

II

The Grantor reserves and shall have the exclusive right at any time and from time to time during his/her lifetime by instrument in writing signed by the Grantor and delivered to the Trustee to modify or alter this Agreement, in whole or in part, without the consent of the Trustee or any beneficiary provided that the duties, powers and liabilities of the Trustee shall not be changed without his/her consent; and the Grantor reserves and shall have the right during his/her lifetime, by instrument in writing, signed by the Grantor and delivered to the Trustee, to cancel and annul this Agreement without the consent of the Trustee or any beneficiary hereof. Grantor expressly reserves the right to appoint successor trustees, replace present trustees and change the beneficiaries or the rights to property due any beneficiary.

III

In addition to any powers granted under applicable law or otherwise, and not in limitation of such powers, but subject to any rights and powers which may be reserved expressly by the Grantor(s) in this Agreement, the Trustee(s) is/are authorized to exercise the following powers in their sole and absolute discretion.

a. To hold and retain any or all property, real, personal, or mixed, received from the Grantor's estate, or from any other source, regardless of any law or rule of court relating to diversification, or non-productivity, for such time as the Trustee shall deem best, and to dispose of such property by sale, exchange, or otherwise, as and when they shall deem advisable; notwithstanding this provision or any other contained herein.

b. To sell, assign, exchange, transfer, partition and convey, or otherwise dispose of, any property, real, personal or mixed, which may be included in or may at any time become part of the Trust Estate, upon such terms and conditions as deemed advisable, at either public or private sale, including options and sales on credit and for the purpose of selling, assigning, exchanging, transferring, partitioning or conveying the same, to make, execute, acknowledge, and deliver any and all instruments of conveyance, deeds of trust, and assignments in such form and with such warranties and covenants as they may deem expedient and proper; and in the event of any sale, conveyance or other disposition of any of the Trust Estate, the purchaser shall not be obligated in any way to see the application of the purchase money or other consideration passing in connection therewith.

c. To lease or rent and manage any or all of the real estate, which may be included in or at any time become a part of the Trust Estate, upon such terms and conditions deemed advisable, irrespective of whether the term of the lease shall exceed the period permitted by law or the probable period of any trust created hereby, and to review and modify such leases; and for the purpose of leasing said real estate, to make, execute, acknowledge and deliver any and all instruments in such form and with such covenants and warranties as they may deem expedient and proper; and to make any repairs, replacements, and improvements, structural and otherwise, of any property, and to charge the expense thereof in an equitable manner to principal or income, as deemed proper.

d. To borrow money for any purpose in connection with said Trust created hereby, and to execute promissory notes or other obligation for amounts so borrowed, and to secure the payment of any such amounts by mortgage or pledge or any real or personal property, and to renew or extend the time of payment of any obligation, secured or unsecured, payable to or by any trust created hereby, for such periods of time as deemed advisable.

e. To invest and reinvest or leave temporarily uninvested any or all of the funds of the Trust Estate as said Trustees in their sole discretion may deem best, including investments in stocks, common and preferred, and common trust fund, without being restricted to those investments expressly approved by statute for investment by fiduciaries, and to change investments from realty to personality, and vice versa.

f. To compromise, adjust, arbitrate, sue or defend, abandon, or otherwise deal with and settle claims, in favor of or against the Trust Estate as the Trustees shall deem best and their decision shall be conclusive.

g. To determine in a fair and reasonable manner whether any part of the Trust Estate, or any addition or increment thereto be income or principal, or whether any cost, charge, expense, tax, or assessment shall be charged against income or principal, or partially against income and partially against principal.

h. To engage and compensate, out of principal or income or both, as equitably determined, agents, accountants, brokers, attorneys-in-fact, attorneys-at-law, tax specialists, realtors, custodians, investment counsel, and other assistants and advisors, and to do so without liability for any neglect, omission, misconduct, or default of any such agent or such agent or professional representative, provided he or she was selected and retained with reasonable care.

i. To vote any stock, bonds, or other securities held by the Trust at any meetings of stockholders, bondholders, or other security holders and to delegate the power so to vote to attorneys-in-fact or proxies under power of attorney, restricted or unrestricted, and to join in or become a party to any organization, readjustment, voting trust, consideration or exchange, and to deposit securities with any persons, and to pay any fees incurred in connection therewith, and to charge the same to principal or income, as deemed proper, and to exercise all of the rights with regard to such securities.

j. To purchase securities, real estate, or other property from the executor or other personal representative of the Grantor's estate, the executor or other personal representative of the Grantor's husband's/wife's estate, and the Trustees of any agreement or declaration executed by the Grantor during his/her lifetime under his/her last will in case his/her executors or Trustees are in need of cash, liquid assets, or income-producing assets with which to pay taxes, claims, or other estate or trust indebtedness, or in case such executors or Trustees are in need of such property to properly exercise and discharge their discretion with respect to distributions to beneficiaries as provided for under such bills, declarations, or agreements. Such purchase may be in cash or may be in exchange for other property of this Trust, and the Trustees shall not be liable in any way for any loss resulting to the Trust Estate by reason of the exercise of said authority.

k. To undertake such further acts as are incidental to any of the foregoing or are reasonably required to carry out the tenor, purpose and intent of the Trust.

l. To make loans or advancements to the executor or other personal representative of the Grantor's estate, the executor or other personal representative of the Grantor's husband's/wife's estate, and the Trustees of any agreement or declaration executed by the Grantor during his/her lifetime or under his/her last will in case such executors or Trustees are in need of cash for any reason. Such loans or advancements may be secured or unsecured, and the Trustees shall not be liable in any way for any loss resulting to the Trust Estate by reason of the exercise of this authority.

IV

Upon death of the Grantor, or the last surviving Grantor if more than one, the remaining Trust assets shall be distributed to the beneficiaries in the proportionate or allocable amounts as are specified in the schedule of beneficiaries as may then be in force.

If any beneficiary and the Grantor should die under such circumstances as would render it doubtful whether the beneficiary or the Grantor died first, then it shall be conclusively presumed for the purposes of this Trust that said beneficiary predeceased the Grantor.

V

If it shall be determined that any provision of the Trust created herein violates any rule against perpetuities or remoteness of vesting now or hereafter in effect in a governing jurisdiction, that portion of the Trust herein created shall be administered as herein provided until the termination of the maximum period allowed by law at which time and forthwith such part of the Trust shall be distributed in fee simple to the beneficiaries then entitled to receive income therefrom, and for the purpose, it shall be presumed that any beneficiary entitled to receive support or education from the income or principal of any particular fund is entitled to receive the income therefrom.

VI

Except as otherwise provided herein, all payments of principal and income payable, or to become payable, to the beneficiary of any trust created hereunder shall not be subject to anticipation, assignment, pledge, sale or transfer in any manner, nor shall any said beneficiary have the power to anticipate or encumber such interest, nor shall such interest, while in possession of the Trustee, be liable for, or subject to, the debts, contracts obligations, liabilities or torts of any beneficiary.

VII

This Trust Agreement shall be construed, regulated and governed by and in accordance with the laws of the State of .

I certify that I have read the foregoing Trust Agreement and that it correctly states the terms and conditions under which the Trust Estate is to be held, managed and disposed of by the Trustee.

Dated:_____________________________ _____________________________________
Grantor

____
Trustee

State of }
County of

On before me, , appeared
personally known to me (or proved to me on the basis of satisfactory evidence) to be the person(s) whose name(s) is/are subscribed to the within instrument and acknowledged to me that he/she/they executed the same in his/her/their authorized capacity(ies), and that by his/her/their signature(s) on the instrument the person(s), or the entity upon behalf of which the person(s) acted, executed the instrument.
WITNESS my hand and official seal.

Signature_____________________________________

Affiant _____Known _____Produced ID
Type of ID_________________________
(Seal)

(Revised 3/93)

K105-3E

REVOCATION OF TRUST

We, the undersigned, , as Settlors/Grantors of a certain revocable living trust entitled , dated , 19 , do hereby revoke said trust effective this date.

1. Notice: A copy of this revocation has been mailed to the below-named trustee(s).

And a further copy of this revocation has been mailed to the below-named beneficiaries.

2. Recording: A signed original of this notice of revocation shall or has been duly recorded with the county recorders office in the following counties:

We make this revocation under oath and affirm that the facts stated herein are true and correct this day of , 19 .

______________________________	______________________________
Settlor/Grantor	Settlor/Grantor

State of }

County of

On before me, ,
appeared
personally known to me (or proved to me on the basis of satisfactory evidence) to be the person(s) whose name(s) is/are subscribed to the within instrument and acknowledged to me that he/she/they executed the same in his/her/their authorized capacity(ies), and that by his/her/their signature(s) on the instrument the person(s), or the entity upon behalf of which the person(s) acted, executed the instrument.

WITNESS my hand and official seal.

Signature_________________________________

Affiant _____Known _____Produced ID

Type of ID_______________________

(Seal)

(Revised 3/93)

K105-4B

SCHEDULE OF ASSETS

Name of Trust:	Date of Trust:

No.	Date of Transfer In	Assets Transferred to Trust	Form of Ownership	Tax Base at Time of Transfer	Fair Market Value on Date of Transfer

K105-5A

No.	Date of Transfer Out	Assets Transferred From Trust	Form of Ownership	Tax Base at Time of Transfer	Fair Market Value on Date of Transfer

The undersigned Grantors have reviewed the Schedule of Assets and approve the form of ownership of property as set forth above this date:

Signature of Grantor/Settlor

Signature of Grantor/Settlor

SCHEDULE OF BENEFICIARIES AND DISTRIBUTIVE SHARES

The following are the named beneficiaries of the
Trust, as of this day of
, 19 .

Name of Beneficiary	Property Distributed and Quantity and/or Percent